Deadliest Diseases
of All Time

The Plague

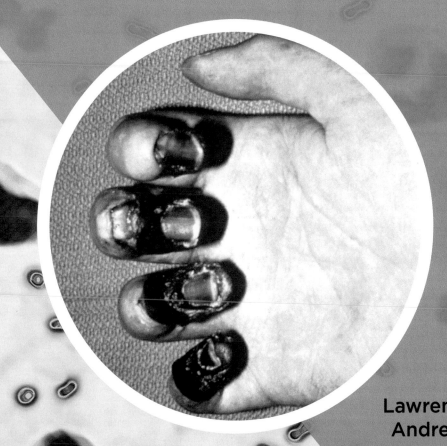

Lawrence
Andrews

Published in 2015 by Cavendish Square Publishing, LLC
243 5th Avenue, Suite 136, New York, NY 10016

CPSIA Compliance Information: Batch #WW15CSQ

All websites were available and accurate when this book was sent to press.

Library of Congress Cataloging-in-Publication Data

Andrews, Lawrence, 1955- author.
The plague / Lawrence Andrews.
    pages cm. — (Deadliest diseases of all time)
Includes bibliographical references and index.
ISBN 978-1-50260-087-5 (hardcover) ISBN 978-1-50260-086-8 (ebook)
1. Plague—History—Juvenile literature. I. Title.

RC172.A53 2015
616.9'232—dc23

                    2014024961

Editor: Kristen Susienka
Senior Copy Editor: Wendy A. Reynolds
Art Director: Jeffrey Talbot
Senior Designer: Amy Greenan
Senior Production Manager: Jennifer Ryder-Talbot
Production Editor: David McNamara
Photo Researcher: J8 Media

The photographs in this book are used by permission and through the courtesy of: Cover photo and page 1, CDC/File:Acral
gangrene due to plague.jpg/Wikimedia Commons; Cover photo and page 1, BSIP/Universal Images Group/Getty Images; Horse
Crazy/Shutterstock.com, 4; De Agostini Picture Library/Getty Images, 7; De Agostini Picture Library/Getty Images, 8; SCIEPRO/
Science Photo Library/Getty Images, 10; Josse Lieferinxe/The Bridgeman Art Library/Getty Images, 12; Nicole Duplaix/
Photolibrary/Getty Images, 13; DEA/A. Dagli Orti/De Agostini/Getty Images, 17; NYPL/Science Source/Photo Researchers/
Getty Images, 18; INTERFOTO/Sammlung Rauch/Mary Evans, 22; Andy85719/File:Bubonic plague-en.svg/Wikimedia
Commons, 25; NYPL/Science Source/Photo Researchers/Getty Images, 27; File:Shibasaburo Kitasato.jpg/Wikimedia Commons,
31; Heiko Kiera/Shutterstock.com, 32; Elliot + Fry Photo Co./File:Waldemar Haffkine.jpg/Wikimedia Commons, 34; Wolfgang
Sauber/File:Naturns St.Proculus-Museum - Pestfriedhof 1.jpg/Wikimedia Commons, 35; Kyslynskyy/iStock/Thinkstock, 38;
CDC National Center for Emerging and Zoonotic Infectious Diseases/Division of VectorBorne Infectious Diseases, 39; CDC/
Courtesy of Larry Stauffer, Oregon State Public Health Laboratory/File:Yersinia pestis fluorescent.jpeg/Wikimedia Commons,
40; worldswildlifewonders/Shutterstock.com, 42; Rodd100/Shutterstock.com, 45; Alexander Raths/iStock/Thinkstock, 49; Zsolt
Biczo/Shutterstock.com, 50; Joolz/File:Bin.JPG/Wikimedia Commons, 52; AP Photo/Tannen Maury, 56.

Printed in the United States of America

Contents

Introduction

Do you have a pet, such as a dog, a cat, or a rat? Chances are that if you lived in Europe in the 1300s, your pet would have been feared and accused of bringing a terrible illness known as the Black Plague to everyone you knew and loved. This disease spread very quickly and came from **bacteria** living inside fleas on rodents. The fleas would bite dogs or cats, which could spread the disease to humans. From there, people passed it on by touching infected animals or breathing the air of a person suffering from plague pneumonia. It killed people very quickly. For instance, a healthy person could go to sleep one night and be dead the next morning.

The disease did not originate in Europe. Beforehand, it had affected people in China, Egypt, and India, and no one knew how to stop it. The plague that struck Asia and Europe during the fourteenth century is known as the Black Plague, or the Black

In medieval times, cats and dogs were thought to bring plague to humans.

Death. The name comes from the large black dots that covered a person's skin.

The Black Plague is one of the most important and devastating events in European and Asian history. It killed approximately 20 million people in Europe and many others throughout the rest of the known world at that time. Some areas of Europe were so devastated that there were not enough people left to bury the dead. Entire generations were wiped out by what was thought to be one disease. Today's historians believe more than one **strain** of the disease killed these huge amounts of people, though.

Parents sent their children to other parts of the world, where they thought they would be safe. However, the plague seemed to follow them. As one child wrote in 1348:

A few months after my sister and I arrived in Paris, the plague struck there, too. This time, I stayed to witness its terrible devastation. My sister soon became ill. It started with a headache and chills, and soon she had growths the size of eggs under the skin on her legs. My sister passed away within three days of getting the plague. My cousins fell victim to the plague as well. I feared that the plague would continue to ravage the city until no one was left.

Eventually, a way of combatting the disease was found, but even today the disease exists. According to

This painting from the fifteenth century shows a man praying before St. Sebastian for protection from the plague.

the **World Health Organization (WHO)**, each year between 1,000 and 2,000 cases of the **bubonic plague** are reported around the world. The highest number of cases occur in Africa, though a few also appear in the western United States and other areas of the world. Advances in medicine and research have allowed us to learn that plagues, as well as other illnesses, have direct scientific causes. This knowledge helps us discover ways of avoiding and limiting the illness.

How did this disease begin, and how did humanity fight it? To answer these questions, we must first understand what the plague is.

one The Facts

When you think of the plague, what comes to mind? A painting from the Middle Ages? A rat? The image of the Grim Reaper, which originated during the Black Death? Plagues are one of the most frightening diseases that affect humanity. If not treated early, they can lead to a widespread global threat of disfigurement and death.

The word "plague" is taken from the Latin word *plaga*, meaning "wound" or "pestilence." A pestilence is a prevalent disease affecting many people in a certain area. This is also called an **epidemic**. One type of plague that affected the Middle Ages and continues to impact people today is called the bubonic plague. It can be either epidemic or **pandemic**, meaning it affects many people around the world.

At the time of the Black Death, it was believed that there was a single, deadly plague. However, that

Doctors had many ways of treating plague victims, as this painting from the fifteenth century illustrates.

Lymph nodes, highlighted in red, help fight infections in the body.

view has changed over the years as historians study the accounts of people who lived through the event. When people suffer from the same illness, they will also suffer from similar symptoms. While the bubonic plague is the form that is most often described in written accounts, there are also written accounts of symptoms that are not characteristic of the bubonic form. These non-bubonic symptoms are believed to have been caused by other forms of plague. This means that more than one plague could have resulted in so many deaths.

It Starts with Bacteria

The bubonic plague is caused by bacteria. Bacteria are microscopic organisms, meaning they are so small you can see them only by examining them under a microscope. A microbiologist studies microscopic organisms. The study of bacteria is a very important science because there are many different kinds of bacteria, and each kind has its own unique effect on other living organisms.

At any time, there are millions of bacteria (the singular form is called bacterium) living around, on, and inside of us. Some types of bacteria are harmless, while others can cause disease and even death. Some forms of harmless bacteria help the body to perform important functions, such as digesting food. Harmful bacteria, however, can cause sore throats, infections, and cavities in teeth. Some also release poisons that cause a variety of symptoms, including the swollen **lymph nodes** of the bubonic plague.

When a harmful bacteria enters the human body through a wound or opening, many antibodies and white blood cells, the body's main lines of defense against illness and disease, attack it. Sometimes they destroy it, while other times the bacteria disguises itself and enters through another way. This is the case with the bacteria that led to bubonic plague. The bubonic plague bacterium takes over the white blood cells and travels to the lymph nodes where it unleashes its poison.

A Closer History

541–544 CE Justinian's plague ravages northern Africa, western Asia, and southern Europe.

1334 The Black Plague occurs in Asia.

1335–1345 The Black Plague is carried west along the Silk Road into western Asia and the Middle East.

1347 The Black Plague strikes the Italian peninsula.

1348 The plague spreads to France, England, Ireland, and Germany.

1349 The Black Plague is carried to Norway and Scotland.

1351 The plague strikes Russia.

1352 The plague forms a deadly ring around Europe.

1893 An outbreak of the plague in China starts the modern pandemic.

Alexandre Yersin, discoverer of the plague bacteria.

1894 Shibasaburo Kitasato and Alexandre Yersin discover the organism that causes bubonic plague.

1896 The first plague **vaccine** is invented by Waldemar Haffkine.

1925 The last urban outbreak of the plague occurs in the United States.

2013 A squirrel in California tests positive for bubonic plague; shuts down parts of Angeles National Forest.

Lymph nodes—also called lymph glands—are located in various parts of our bodies. Some can be felt just beneath the skin, while others are found deep inside the body. Lymph nodes hold special cells that destroy and kill bacteria and viruses that get into the body. The bubonic plague causes an infected person's lymph nodes to swell, sometimes becoming as large as an egg or an apple. The most common area of swelling from the plague is in the groin area, which is how the bubonic plague was named—the Greek word for "groin" is *boubon*. Other noticeable swellings can occur in the lymph nodes of the armpits and on the back of the neck.

The Bringer of Plague

The bacterium that causes the bubonic plague is called *Yersinia pestis*. This bacterium is named after Alexandre Émile John Yersin, the Swiss microbiologist who discovered it. In 1894, there was a violent outbreak of the bubonic plague in Hong Kong. Yersin, who was working in French Indochina (present-day Vietnam, Laos, and Cambodia), hurried to Hong Kong and set up a temporary laboratory. He examined the bodies of people who had died of the plague. By studying tissue samples that he took from the buboes, or swollen lymph glands, and organs of the deceased victims, he was able to locate the **microorganism** that caused the plague. Yersin published his findings later that year.

However, he was not the only one trying to discover the origins of the plague. At the same time, another microbiologist named Shibasaburo Kitasato published his own findings on the bacteria. Although history debates which man was first to isolate the "bringer of plague," many people feel that Yersin's research findings are more accurate than Kitasato's findings; therefore, Yersin receives the credit today. For many years, the bacteria was called *Pasteurella bacilla* after the Pasteur Institute of Paris, where Yersin had been a student and lab assistant. Today, *Yersinia pestis* is the accepted name for the bacteria in the medical community.

Types of Plague

There are three types of plague. Each of them are caught in different ways and have slightly different characteristics.

Bubonic plague is perhaps the most well known. People usually catch it through flea bites. The most common feature is the "bubo," or swelling of certain glands in the body. The lymph nodes and groin are particularly sensitive to swelling, too.

Septicemic plague can also be the first symptom of other plagues. People develop large pustules on the skin—usually on the fingers, toes, and nose—that turn black. Sometimes people's limbs can fall off as a result of this. A person catches this form of plague from untreated bubonic plague, flea bites, or touching infected animals.

Pneumonic plague is the most severe strain. A person may develop it from untreated bubonic or septicemic plague, or from breathing in droplets of other infected people's coughs. According to the Centers for Disease Control and Prevention (CDC), it is "the only form of plague that can be spread from person to person (by infectious droplets)."

Do I Have the Plague?

You might wonder, "How do I know if I have the plague?" Just like each form of plague differs slightly, so do the symptoms. All forms of the disease bring some sort of fever, chills, and weakness. There may also be vomiting and diarrhea. However, specific forms of plague have specific characteristics. Pneumonic plague also involves severe pneumonia, and septicemic plague can lead to bleeding of the skin or internal organs.

Why So Long?

Before Yersin's discovery, many people speculated on the disease's origins. Some people thought it had appeared to signal the end of the world, while others thought it was God's punishment on humanity. Throughout history, episodes of the plague came and went, and only the most severe outbreaks are remembered today.

Why did it take so long to discover where it came from? The answer is simple. People did not have the

In the 1300s, many religious men and women cared for and treated victims of the plague.

resources or scientific advancements to get to the bottom of the illness. When the plague first arrived in China in the 1300s, no one knew what it was or how it got there. They couldn't look it up in a book or on the Internet. However, there were many early attempts to combat the disease. These included techniques such as holding a chicken under a person's arm, popping every one of the sores on a person's body to drain the disease from them, and killing all cats and dogs in an infected village. However, these practices died out in time. By the Chinese outbreak in the late 1800s, humanity's advancements in medicine allowed Yersin's landmark discovery to change the path of the disease and all that humans knew about it forever.

Travels of a Deadly Disease

Ever since humans learned how to record written history, accounts of illnesses and plagues devastating populations have also been found. Some historians believe one of the earliest written accounts of the bubonic plague is in the Bible's Old Testament. A Bible passage in the First Book of Samuel describes a group called the Philistines, who had stolen a sacred object called the Ark of the Covenant from the Israelites. They suffered from an outbreak of tumors or sores not long after stealing it. They decided to give the Ark of the Covenant back, and sent along with it statues of rodents and tumors. Soon after, seventy Israelites also died of causes similar to how some of the Philistines had died. Since signs of rodents and tumors appear in the story, and archaeological evidence supporting the presence of one of the varieties of fleas that infects people has been discovered in the area, many agree this could be an early-recorded instance of the plague.

The Black Plague changed thoughts of death. Once a peaceful sleep, it was now a terrible enemy, as this image of Death chasing Londoners during the plague in the sixteenth century shows.

By studying other writings from different eras in history, historians have created a type of timeline of the disease.

Pandemic Spreads Panic—541 CE

Historians believe that the first worldwide, or pandemic, plague occurred in the sixth century. During this time, the Byzantine Empire was ruled by a man named Justinian, which is why this plague is often called Justinian's plague. Much of our knowledge about this plague is taken from the writings of a legal advisor named Procopius. Procopius was traveling on a series of missions throughout the Mediterranean during the time of the pandemic outbreak.

Procopius wrote in *History of the Wars* that the plague started in Pelusium, which was an Egyptian city at the easternmost mouth of the Nile River. The plague then swept westward across Mediterranean Europe. People from Constantinople to Spain were ravaged. Procopius observed that all of the victims of the plague suffered the same symptoms. His writings mention the bubo swellings in the armpits, groin, and neck areas.

Many people thought God was punishing them. According to Procopius, people flocked to religious places in the hope that being near God would spare them. However, there was no escape. Men and women, young and old, all people could become infected. The disease did not discriminate. Eventually, Procopius stated, people shut their doors and let no one in. Doctors of that time were puzzled. How had the disease begun, and how had it spread? Some of the physicians examined the bodies of those who had died and determined that many had died quickly, while others had suffered.

In Constantinople, the capital of the Byzantine Empire, the bodies of plague victims were so numerous that disposing of them became a problem in itself. Some were burned, while others were buried in mass graves or thrown into bodies of water. In many areas the number of corpses became so great that many were simply placed on rooftops while others were left to rot in their homes.

Historians now believe that Justinian's plague originated in central Africa, rather than in Pelusium itself. The epidemic is believed to have been carried northward, through Pelusium and into Europe. Even after the pandemic plague ceased, occasional plague outbreaks occurred throughout the Mediterranean region during the rest of the sixth century.

Taking It to the Extreme— Medieval Times

The next major outbreak is perhaps the most well known and remembered. It is one of the worst plagues ever to strike humanity. The Black Plague, as it came to be called, first began in China in 1334. When it eventually subsided, millions of people in Europe and around the world had died, and thousands of communities were devastated.

Fourteenth Century Medical Practices

Before the Black Plague struck, people held various beliefs as to why illness occurred. Most people's beliefs about illness were based on myths and superstitions. Some people believed that bad **vapors**, or clouds of gas, were the cause of illness. Others thought the body's **humors**, or fluids, were imbalanced. It was also believed that illness developed as a form of divine wrath, or punishment from God.

This image depicts the concept of humors, or fluids, being removed from the body to restore a person's balance of health.

In the fourteenth century, medicine was still a primitive practice. Most medical treatments were based on the idea that the body contained excess fluids that needed to be released. Many of these treatments were quite painful, and in most cases did the patient more harm than good. One popular treatment, called bloodletting, was often performed in order to balance the fluids of an ill patient. The patient was cut and

The Plague

allowed to bleed into a bowl. Blood was drained until the patient felt faint. In some cases, bloodletting was done through the use of bloodsucking leeches.

Another common treatment was called cupping. Doctors heated cups and placed them on the skin of the infected patient. As the cups cooled, suction was created. The suction of the cooling cups caused the skin under the cup to become swollen. The swollen areas of skin were believed to be filled with excess body fluids. By bringing the extra fluids to the surface, health was expected to improve. Neither bloodletting nor cupping was an effective treatment for illness. Not surprisingly, many patients who underwent such treatments died anyway.

Not all treatments were as painful as bloodletting and cupping. Medieval doctors also gave herbal tonics, or potions, to their patients. It was believed that every substance found in nature had a powerful and sometimes healing property. Doctors mixed tonics out of hundreds of substances, including such strange things as earthworms, dirt, and urine. Most of these tonics had little medical value, and some were dangerous or even deadly.

Other treatments for illness were of a religious nature. Many people believed that if they prayed to God, the punishment of illness would be lifted. Ill people would also take pilgrimages, or trips, to sacred places such as the Holy Land, present-day Palestine and

Israel, in the hope that they would be cured. However, movement to other places only spread the diseases.

The Black Death Arrives

Historians believe that the Black Death started in Asia and then spread westward into Europe. This plague eventually killed two-thirds of China's inhabitants. The plague then spread west across China, through the Middle East, and into the countries along the eastern Mediterranean. The plague spread along the trade routes, such as the Silk Road from China and the Rhine trade routes of Europe. It spread freely by ship and by land, wherever there was a source of people or rats to carry the disease.

The plague first reached Europe, or more specifically the Italian peninsula, in 1347. It was brought to Italy by merchant ships that had returned from Kaffa, a Genoese trading port on the Black Sea. An army that wished to drive the Genoese out of Kaffa had been attacking the port.

When the attacking army developed the plague, they catapulted the infected corpses of their soldiers over the walls and into Kaffa. The Genoese dumped the infected bodies into the water as quickly as possible, but it was too late. The plague set in at Kaffa, infecting the people who lived there.

Hoping to escape the plague that was spreading throughout Kaffa, four Genoese ships returned to the Italian peninsula. Tragically, the four ships were

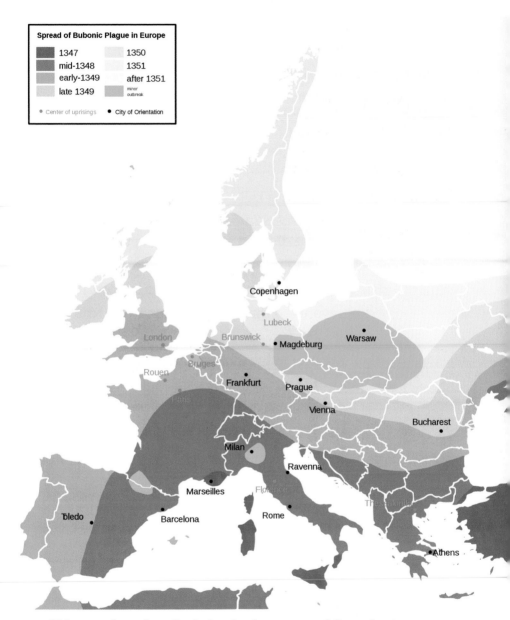

This map shows how the bubonic plague spread throughout Europe during the fourteenth century.

Doctor Death

While many doctors and other officials known for helping members of society, such as priests, refused to take care of people when the Black Plague settled over Europe, a few braved the streets and the homes of the ill. Some took advantage of families, charging them extra money to tend to their dying relatives, or offering false hope where there was nothing to do but wait. Many times, they simply counted the bodies as they piled up in the streets.

Later, when the disease reappeared in the 1600s, physicians of the era who tended to the sick and dying were well equipped (or so they thought) to prevent the disease from spreading to them. They wore theatrical-looking outfits meant to protect the mouth, eyes, and face from the illness. These outfits consisted of a heavy gown made of leather and coated in wax, a kind of gas mask with a bird's beak, goggles, and a brimmed hat. Inside the beak was usually a strong-smelling herb or perfume meant to purify the air around the "plague doctor," as he was called. In addition to wearing the costume, doctors carried long sticks to keep the patients at arm's length.

The inventor of this costume is thought to be a Frenchman named Charles de l'Orme, who lived in the seventeenth century. He tended to royalty and other influential people in France who had caught the plague, people he couldn't refuse helping. To combat the disease, he created the outfit, though there is no evidence the suit kept the disease out.

There have been several noteworthy plague doctors since. Having perhaps one of the briefest careers as a plague doctor was John Paulitious, the first plague doctor in Edinburgh, Scotland. When an outbreak occurred there in 1645, Paulitious was the first to attend to men and women in Edinburgh's city center. Unfortunately, he died shortly after starting his visits, having become a victim of the disease.

contaminated with the plague. When the ships docked, most of the sailors were dead, and there was no stopping the plague from entering Italy.

From its foothold on the Italian peninsula, the plague quickly spread northward into central Europe. By 1348, the populations of Paris, England, Ireland, and Germany were being ravaged by the disease. It was carried farther north into Norway and Scotland in 1349 and east into Russia two years later. By 1352, the plague had almost formed a complete circle around Europe, reaching the Russian city of Kiev, which was located just 435 miles (700 km) north of Kaffa. For the next four centuries, the plague reappeared in smaller outbreaks throughout Eurasia, made up of Europe and Asia, every twenty years or so.

Concepts of Illness and Death Change

Before the occurrence of the Black Plague, death was often viewed as the final part of life before joining God. Before the plague, literature and art often compared death to a kind friend or gentle being. After the plague years, literature and art reflected the attitude that death was a painful and cruel enemy. Many paintings of the time show the character of death as a frightening and horrid figure.

The Disease Stirs Violence

The cause of the Black Death was not known during the time it was devastating the towns and cities of fourteenth century Europe. This ignorance filled people with fear and led to wild speculation and false beliefs about the cause of the plague. Many people absurdly came to believe that the plague had been started by the Jews. It was believed that Jews deliberately created the plague because they wanted to destroy Christians. This belief grew out of centuries of prejudice against Jews.

Jews were accused of poisoning the water, which was believed to have caused the sickness. This accusation led to the persecution and murder of many innocent Jews. Many Jews were taken captive and tortured until they agreed that they had poisoned the water.

During the course of the plague, thousands of Jews were exiled from or murdered in Germany, Belgium, Holland, and other parts of Europe. In Strasbourg, more than two thousand Jews were told to convert to Christianity. Those who refused were tied to stakes and burned to death. Small children were pulled from the fire and baptized as the parents died. In some villages, Jews set their own houses on fire and killed themselves.

Despite all the panic, fear, and hatred that spurred from the Black Death, the course of history itself altered and became an opportunity for survivors to create new lives for themselves once the disease had run its course. In its aftermath, two-thirds of Europe's population had been destroyed, and those left behind needed to create new societies. In the new Europe, peasants could aspire to become merchants, hierarchies were rearranged, and overall lives changed and improved for some. Many argue the disease is responsible for the Renaissance era that dominated the 1600s and 1700s.

Return of the Plague— The Nineteenth Century

The third great pandemic started in the south of China in 1893. This outbreak of the plague was spread by caravan and river routes to the great Chinese cities of Hong Kong and Canton. By 1896, it had spread west into the cities of Singapore and Bombay. The plague was also carried south into the Malay Peninsula and the Philippine Islands. Far-reaching trade routes carried the plague from southern Asia to Europe, Africa, North and South America, and Australia. By 1900, cities as far from China as Buenos Aires, Rio de Janeiro, and San Francisco experienced outbreaks of the plague.

It's estimated that 25 million people died over the course of the next seventy-five years from the pandemic and the occasional plague outbreaks that followed. It was during this outbreak of the plague that Alexandre Yersin and Shibasaburo Kitasato discovered the organism that causes the disease. At the time, it wasn't known that fleas can transmit the plague from infected rats to humans. However, a physician named Mary Miles observed that rats in China were struck with the plague as well as humans. It was also noted that rats

Shibasaburo Kitasato was one of the first men to identify the bacteria responsible for the Black Plague.

came out of their holes in broad daylight, stumbled about as if in a daze, and then died. This led to further study, which encouraged scientists around the world to investigate the cause of the disease. Eventually, in the late 1800s, Waldemar Mordecai Haffkine invented the first plague vaccine.

How did he do this? What steps were taken afterward that led to today's preventative techniques? The answers can be understood if we first study how the disease passes between animals and humans.

three Passing on the Plague

By the time of the Hong Kong pandemic in the late 1800s, physicians and microbiologists of the day had observed the disease firsthand and had drawn some conclusions as to why it happened. First, they knew the plague was sparked by some sort of germ. What was unknown was how the germ got into the human body. Some thought the germ lived in food, or came from open wounds. There were many campaigns around the world to disinfect cities. Chemicals were placed into sewers as one method. This, in fact, drove rats from the sewers in which they lived farther into the cities, causing the disease to spread more.

Research Discovers the Cause

Around the same time that Yersin and Kitasato published their findings on the plague, a Japanese physician named Masanori Ogata recommended

Rats and other rodents are largely responsible for carrying the *Yersinia pestis* bacteria.

others to look to the fleas on rats. He noticed that when the rats died, the fleas left their bodies. Then, in 1898, a man named Paul-Louis Simond published his findings on the disease. He stated for the first time that fleas on rats bit people and transferred the plague to them. Unfortunately, the public or medical professionals did not take his claims seriously at that time, since people did not believe fleas attacked humans.

Waldemar Haffkine, inventor of first plague vaccine.

Soon after, Waldemar Haffkine invented the first vaccine for the plague. He did this by injecting the *Yersinia pestis* bacteria directly into the body. He first tested it on himself, then set up trials in India (which at that time was controlled by Britain) to test it on other people. While side effects included a high fever, the vaccine became widely used around the world. However, it did not mean plague had been defeated forever.

It would take further decades of study before the current method of treatment, a plague **antibiotic**, was discovered and the behavior of *Yersinia pestis* fully understood. Today, we know a lot more about how the bacteria functions once inside the human body, and how it transfers from animals to humans, causing widespread fear and, in some cases, death.

The Life of Bacteria

As you have read, the cause of this disease is a microscopic organism. A bacterium is a living thing that, like you and me, wants to survive however it can. For bacteria to survive, they need to live in a place where they will feel protected and where they can multiply. They also need elements that will sustain them, like sugar, vitamins, chemicals, and minerals. Many of these **nutrients** are found in living organisms: plants, animals, and humans, and sometimes dirt or water. In order to survive, a bacterium needs a host that will give it enough nutrients and a safe place to live. Sometimes humans are that host, other times animals or plants become places where bacteria thrive.

A struggle for life occurs when a bacterium enters a host. The cells and organs of a body work to protect the body from harmful things. Some bacteria are allowed to survive in a host body because the body knows that

This skeleton was unearthed in a cemetery for plague victims. Many people are worried that the same, or a new, strain of the bacteria will appear to kill more people.

Past Problems Form Future Worries

Some health professionals today worry that the disease could reappear in a different, antibiotic- and vaccine-resistant strain. Recent studies on the DNA of victims of the Justinian Plague in 500 CE seem to show a slightly different version of the same bubonic plague that killed almost two-thirds of the population in the Middle Ages. If the disease evolves in modern times into a new strain, it could greatly affect the world's population again.

those bacteria are harmless. Bacteria that are harmful or damaging to the host, however, are selected by the body to be killed. Most bacteria want to keep their host alive because the body is their source for nutrition. Harmful bacteria will cause infections, illness, and death despite the fact that they need to keep their host alive. Harmful bacteria produce and release poisons, or toxins, into the body, which can cause any number of symptoms.

In order to get into the body of a host, bacteria must come into contact with the host. Different kinds of bacteria can come into contact with a host in different ways. Here are a few examples:

1. By Eating Bad Food or Water

A host can be infected with bacteria by consuming contaminated food or water. Bacteria live in the contaminated food and water, and when we consume it, we allow the bacteria into our bodies. Contaminated food and water help to transmit the bacteria into our bodies.

2. By Breathing

Bacteria can also be transmitted to a host through dust and liquid droplets in the air. Liquid droplets can be found in your breath. A person infected with certain kinds of bacteria can transmit them to you through his or her breath by coughing or sneezing.

3. By Touching

Bacteria can enter a host through direct contact. Bacteria can enter through scratches or openings in the

Badgers are among the many animals that can carry the plague bacteria and transmit it to the fleas that bite humans.

skin. The bacteria can be on or in any person, animal, or item that the host handles or has direct physical contact with.

4. By Being Bitten or Scratched

Bacteria can enter the host by using a **vector**. A vector is another organism or insect that bites or scratches the surface of the skin of the host. When the skin is punctured, the wound can act as a doorway that lets the bacteria into the host. The vector might also deposit a fluid that contains the bacteria.

How the Plague Is Passed On

The bacteria *Yersinia pestis* lives in some wild animals that are carriers of the disease. This means they are resistant to the sickness caused by the bacteria even though the bacteria is inside their bodies. Bears, coyotes, badgers, skunks, and raccoons are examples of wild animals that can carry the bacteria. When fleas bite these wild animals, they drink the bacteria in the animal's blood.

The most common way of transferring the plague is through a vector. Fleas are the vectors most responsible for transmitting the disease between animals and humans. Since fleas need to feed on blood to live,

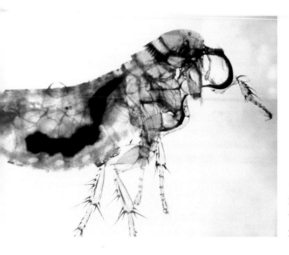

Thrassis bacci johnsoni (pictured here) is one of the fleas capable of carrying the plague bacteria and infecting humans.

they transmit the plague after drinking the blood of an infected rat or other animal. The bacteria multiply and grow so quickly that the flea's gut becomes clogged. When the flea's gut is clogged, it is not able to digest the blood. When the flea bites a new host, it tries to draw blood in but ends up releasing the blood that it could not digest into the new host. The blood that goes into

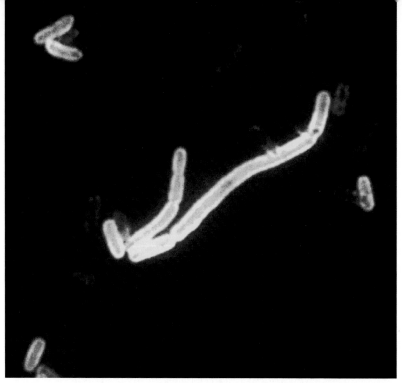

Yersinia pestis, illuminated and magnified in this image, is the bacteria responsible for all varieties of the plague that harm humans.

the new host will carry the *Yersinia pestis* bacteria with it, which in turn infect the new host with the plague.

There are several different **species**, or varieties, of fleas in the world. About 100 flea varieties are known to be carriers of *Yersinia pestis*. Not all of the carrying varieties can pass the bacteria along, or act as vectors of the plague. There are thirty-one varieties of fleas that have been proven to be vectors of the plague.

Humans can contract the disease from animals through a vector or direct physical contact. Once in the human population, the plague can be transmitted from person to person through liquid droplets.

The Beginnings of the Plague

Plague epidemics occur when bacteria spread from infected wild animals to rat or rodent populations. The plague is transmitted from the wild animals to other animals through a vector or through direct physical contact. The rat or rodent populations are not as resistant to the bacteria as the wild animals. The bacteria can cause a plague among the rat or rodent population. Animals such as cats and dogs that come into contact with infected rats and rodents can also become infected.

As the rat or rodent populations die out, the fleas must search for new food sources. Since rat and rodent populations live near humans, humans are often the next source of nutrients for the infected fleas. When the flea finds its human host, it bites through the skin to draw blood. The infected blood that the flea was not able to digest will be released into the human host. The blood carries *Yersinia pestis* through the bite wound and into the new human host.

Yersinia pestis is not immortal, though. According to the CDC, if the bacteria are exposed to sunlight and dry out, they will die. However, if they are released into the air, bacteria can survive for as long as one hour, depending on the conditions into which they are released. Still, the plague is a disease best avoided or treated as quickly as possible if an infection is suspected.

four The Plague in Modern Times

While advancements in medicine and sanitation have led to ways of further fighting and limiting cases of the plague, in some parts of the world the disease and its different forms still claim lives every year. Africa is the nation with the highest number of deaths per year. In the western part of the United States, where more colonies of rats live, some cases of bubonic plague have also been reported. According to the CDC, an average of seven people in the United States contract the disease each year, which is a very low number compared to the world's yearly average of 2,000 cases. Through study and medical development, we now know the way plague is contracted, how to diagnose it, treat it, and even prevent it. However, threats of another outbreak still loom in the backs of people's minds, and world health agencies have detailed steps for what to do in case of an unexpected outbreak.

In the United States, squirrels are sometimes responsible for infecting humans with the plague.

The Plague's Victims

Anybody who has had exposure to plague-infected wild animals can contract the disease. People and animals that come into contact with, or even get near, rodents that have died from the plague are at risk for getting the disease. When an animal dies of the plague, the disease is carried on by the infected fleas that lived on the animal. The fleas, searching for a host body, will jump onto any animal or human that gets close enough. A person can also catch the plague if he or she has scratches or other skin openings, and comes into direct contact with a plague-infected animal or person. House pets can also bring the plague or plague-infested fleas into the home. A person can become infected either through indirect or direct physical contact with an infected house pet.

An example of how easy it is to catch the plague from animals occurred in July 2014. A man living in the city of Yumen in China contracted the plague after touching an animal called a marmot. He soon died from the disease, which sparked a nationwide panic. Government officials forbade all 30,000 residents of the city from leaving, and urged motorists to find other routes of travel. "The city has enough rice, flour, and oil to supply all its residents for up to one month," China Central Television reported. While all citizens were closely monitored, this reaction to the plague highlights just how serious the disease remains today.

The Grey Squirrel and the Black Death

In July 2013, panic swept over the state of California when a squirrel was caught in a routine inspection at a park in Los Angeles. This squirrel, undergoing usual examinations by researchers, tested positive for the bacteria *Yersinia pestis*. As part of an immediate response to the incident, three campgrounds in the Angeles National Park, where the squirrel lived, were closed down. When word of the presumed infected animal caught the eye and ear of the public, many people across the world wondered if this was the start of the next big pandemic. However, health officials from the United States and abroad assured them that this did not mean the return of the Black Death was imminent. They repeated that cases of bubonic plague occur in places around the country, and the world, each year. If treated quickly enough, around 90 percent of people diagnosed survive.

Determining the Disease

Plague infections require an immediate diagnosis, as death from the plague can take place in as little as three days from the time of infection. A doctor attempting to diagnose the disease will look for these classic symptoms:

- A general feeling of sickness
- High fever
- Chills
- Headaches
- Delirium
- Helplessness
- **Hemorrhages** under the skin
- Darkened skin on the hands and legs
- Painful or tender swollen lymph nodes
- White coating on the tongue
- Sensitivity to light

If a doctor suspects that a patient may have the plague, the doctor is required by law to isolate the patient from everyone else. The patient will be hospitalized and undergo laboratory tests. There are different tests for the different forms of the plague. The doctor will have samples of the patient's blood, lymph glands, or saliva examined for presence of the plague bacteria.

If the results show that the patient has the plague, certain steps are taken to keep it from spreading. People who have been in close contact with the patient will be identified and evaluated for the possibility of infection.

All suspected and actual cases of the plague are reported to local and state health departments. Diagnosis of the plague is usually confirmed by the CDC, which reports all U.S. plague cases to the World Health Organization.

Treatments Today

Immediate treatment for the plague is very important in order to ensure the patient's survival. As soon as the plague is suspected, doctors will prescribe an antibiotic for the patient. An antibiotic is a medication that does not allow bacteria to survive and multiply in an infected person. The most common antibiotics given to plague-infected patients are streptomycin and gentamicin. Typically, a patient takes one dose a day for ten days or until two weeks after the fever subsides. This is important, as the plague, especially its pneumonic form, is contagious.

Some antibiotics can also be given before the disease is contracted, as a preventative measure. These antibiotics are called **prophylactic antibiotics**. The word "prophylactic" means protection. Prophylactic antibiotics can keep people from developing the plague if they become exposed to it in the near future. These antibiotics are given to people to protect them from getting the plague, rather than to treat them for plague infection. Prophylactic antibiotics might also be given to anyone who has had, or will have, close exposure to an infected patient. Doctors will also give prophylactic antibiotics to anyone who will be traveling to an area of the world where a plague outbreak is occurring. This will ensure that the person does not become infected with the plague even though he or she is exposed to it.

Today there are two main types of vaccine used to fight plague: live attenuated and formalin-killed. Live attenuated vaccine means that a small amount of the live bacteria is inserted into the body. Formalin-killed vaccine means that the bacteria entering the body has been killed in a liquid such as formaldehyde. These vaccines, however, can have severe side effects and do not protect against all forms of plague, specifically the most severe kind, pneumonic plague.

In the United States, plague vaccine is not available for the public. In many countries, including the United States, a plague vaccine is saved for health professionals in case of an emergency outbreak. If an outbreak of the disease were to happen today, the vaccine would be ineffective in treating the entire population. According to the WHO, this is because "one month or more is required [for a person] to develop a protective immune response." In other words, once the vaccine is injected into a person, it needs about a month or more for the body's defense system to combat it and remember it in case of repeat attacks. Likewise, in order for a person to be vaccinated against the plague, they need to receive multiple shots over a period of many months. Because vaccines take time to work, they cannot be used for

While plague vaccine is not available to the public, some health workers are vaccinated each year with a reserve supply.

immediate protection against the plague. Vaccines are more effective for people who need long-term protection from the plague because they are exposed to it on a regular basis. Scientists who handle and study *Yersinia pestis* and people who handle infected animals as part of their work are among those people who are commonly vaccinated against the plague.

Today's Research

Research continues today on the disease because not everything about it is known, and new information is appearing. As previously mentioned, recent studies of the victims of the Justinian Plague revealed a different strain of the disease evident in those bodies than there was of the victims of the Black Death of the fourteenth century. This has people questioning what the fate of the plague in modern times will be. Will a new strain, resistant to current combative techniques, arise? What does its future hold, and how would humanity cope with another widespread outbreak?

five The Plague of the Future

For centuries, the plague has been a constant shadow for humanity. Since its first recorded appearance in the Bible, it has resurfaced time and time again and has had a deadly effect on societies around the world. Today, however, it can be controlled and avoided thanks to modern advances in medicine, sanitation, and health. What steps are being taken to prevent the spread of the plague? What role do these aspects play in preventing plague from growing out of hand? What does the disease's future look like? Most importantly, what would the future of humanity itself look like if faced with another outbreak?

Keeping the Streets Clean

Outbreaks commonly occur in areas of the world where housing and sanitation conditions are poor. The word "sanitation" means the protection of good health by keeping living conditions clean. Rats and

Preventing plague starts with you. Help keep the world around you clean!

By throwing away your garbage and recycling, you keep rats and other plague-carrying rodents away.

rodents often live in areas where sanitation conditions are poor, and contact with plague-infected rodents is very dangerous to humans.

The very first step that we can take in reducing the risk of being exposed to the plague is to control the number of rodents and fleas in and near the areas where we live. Maintaining good sanitation conditions will ensure that rodents are not drawn to these areas. This is called environmental sanitation. The first step of environmental sanitation is to protect food sources that could attract rats and rodents. By making garbage and pet food sources tamper-proof, we can reduce the number of rodents that will be drawn to them.

The second step of environmental sanitation is to remove all junk piles from areas where people live. These junk piles offer rodents a place to build their nests. By removing the piles, we can make it harder for rodents to find shelter.

There are various poisons that can also be used to keep rodent populations under control. These powerful chemicals should be used only by professionals as they are harmful to humans as well. Using disinfectants and cleaning agents in and around our homes on a regular basis is another way to keep good sanitation conditions.

Staying Aware and Acting on Problems

Although it has been attempted, killing wild animals that may be carriers of the plague is costly and very difficult to do. People who live in areas near wild animal populations that are known to carry the plague should be aware of how to avoid exposure. These people should also keep an eye out for plague activity in local rodent populations. A sure sign of plague activity among rodent populations is a large number of rodent deaths. It is important that people report any cases of sick or dead animals to their local health department or law enforcement agency. Trained professionals who know how to handle the possibility of disease will investigate the animal deaths. Other actions that people can take to ensure that they don't contract the plague are:

- Treating pets with flea control on a regular basis, either through flea collars or flea powders. Pets should also be regularly inspected for fleas.
- Limiting the number of times that pets are allowed to freely roam outdoors.
- Telling authorities immediately if contact is made with a possibly plague-infected animal. If for any reason the animal has to be handled, gloves should always be worn on the hands of

the person handling the animal.

- Wearing flea repellent on skin and clothing when traveling to areas where exposure to the plague is possible.
- Removing junk piles and potential food sources around the home that could attract rodents.
- Wearing gloves and using a strong disinfectant or cleaner while cleaning areas that wild animals have infested. The entire area should be wet with cleaner. Any remains or animal materials should be disposed of in sealed bags.

Be Prepared When Traveling

People who travel to areas where animals or humans are known to have the plague should take precautions to lower their risk of becoming infected. Travelers can take prophylactic antibiotics before their trips to strengthen their resistance to the plague. Travelers should avoid any areas where recent human cases have occurred. People should also avoid areas where dead rats have been found and avoid handling any sick or dead animals from those areas. Bug repellents should be applied to clothing, skin, and bedding accommodations.

An Uncertain Future

While the modern world has not experienced a pandemic on the scales of the Black Death or Hong Kong outbreaks, some scientists think that another strain of the disease could evolve, or *Yersinia pestis* could

Global Action

You are not alone in wanting to keep the plague away from your door. World environmental and health agencies are also taking steps to monitor and treat plague outbreaks around the globe. Both the CDC and WHO have information on their websites dedicated to providing the public with the disease's detailed history and the most up-to-date news, statistics, and information about the plague. These websites also list what measures the agencies themselves are taking in societies today. The WHO has its own Global Alert and Response (GAR) teams that offer emergency medical care to infected communities, and create detailed plans for countries involved in case of plague or other disease epidemics or pandemics.

In areas where plague is known to be, such as parts of the western United States, environmental agencies keep track of rat and other rodent populations. They check animals and animal communities routinely to assess their health and check for any signs of disease, such as the plague. If large amounts of rodents start to die suddenly, health and environmental officials can quickly determine whether or not the mass deaths were caused by plague. If so, they can move quickly to informing and aiding the public.

CDC and WHO workers often wear protective suits like this when visiting places where infectious diseases exist.

be used as a **biological weapon**. The plague is a disease that has not gone away, no matter how many vaccines or antibiotics have been created or other preventative measures have been taken. It still exists and affects people every year. If *Yersinia pestis* were to get into the wrong hands, it could be unleashed on the public and cause panic and severe consequences for the societies involved. Another pandemic of the disease could also ravage the world on a scale not seen before. If current vaccines and antibiotics could not fight it, humanity would be seriously threatened.

It's true that the plague is a deadly disease, one of the worst to affect humans. However, while threats of outbreaks continue to exist, modern medicine will continue to investigate new techniques in preparing for the disease's uncertain future. Their main aim is to protect you, your loved ones, and the rest of the human population.

Glossary

antibiotic Medicine that destroys the growth of bacteria.

bacteria Microorganisms that can be harmful or harmless to other living things.

biological weapon A harmful organism (such as a germ that causes disease) used as a weapon.

bubonic plague A form of the plague where swelling occurs in the lymph glands of the neck, armpit, or groin.

epidemic The sudden breaking out of a disease in a particular area, affecting many people at the same time.

hemorrhage A discharge or release of blood.

humor Any of the four body fluids believed by the Romans and Greeks to influence health and personality.

lymph nodes Infection–fighting centers of the body, also known as lymph glands.

Glossary

microorganism A very small organism, or living thing.

nutrients An ingredient, usually from food, that gives you energy and helps you live.

pandemic The sudden breaking out of a disease in many areas around the world, affecting many people at the same time.

pneumonic plague A form of plague that infects the lungs.

prophylactic antibiotic Any antibiotic that is used to prevent the plague, rather than to treat the plague.

septicemic plague A form of the plague that infects the bloodstream.

species Varieties of an animal or plant.

strain   A disease closely related to but slightly different than another disease.

vaccine   Any substance given to provoke an immune response in humans, e.g., a flu vaccine.

vapor   A cloudy substance in the air.

vector   A transmitter of microorganisms from one animal or species to another.

World Health Organization (WHO)   The body that oversees and manages world health practices and guidelines for the United Nations system.

For More Information

Interested in learning more about the plague? Check out these websites and organizations.

Websites

Brought to Life: The Black Death – The Science Museum UK
www.sciencemuseum.org.uk/broughttolife/themes/diseases/
black_death.aspx

This is an interactive website taking you on a journey through a medieval town, where the Plague dominated during the 1300s.

"Plague" – Centers for Disease Control and Prevention (CDC)
www.cdc.gov/plague

This website created by the CDC details the plague's history, facts, and how you can prevent catching the disease.

Organizations

Centers for Disease Control (CDC)
1600 Clifton Road
Atlanta, GA 30333
(404) 639-3311; (800) 232-4636
Website: www.cdc.gov

The Pan American Health Organization
Regional Office of the World Health Organization
525 Twenty-third Street NW
Washington, DC 20037
(202) 974-3000
Website: www.paho.org

For Further Reading

Barnard, Bryan. *Outbreak!: Plagues That Changed History*. New York, NY: Crown Books for Young Readers, 2005.

Farrell, Jeanette. *Invisible Enemies: Stories of Infectious Diseases*. New York, NY: Farrar, Staus, and Giroux, 2005.

Friedlander, Mark P., Jr. *Outbreak: Disease Detectives at Work*. Minneapolis, MN: Twenty-First Century Books, 2009.

Gupta, Sunetra. *Pandemics: Our Fears and the Facts*. Seattle, WA: Amazon. Kindle Edition, 2013.

Scott, Susan, and Christopher Duncan. *Return of the Black Death*. Hoboken, NJ: Wiley, 2004.

Ziegler, Philip. *The Black Death*. New York, NY: Harper Perennial, 2009.

Index

environmental sanitation, 52

epidemic, 9, 21, 41, 55

fever, 16, 34, 46, 47

flea/bug repellent, 54

fleas, 5, 19, 30, 34, **38**, 39–41, 44, 52–53

Haffkine, Waldemar, 13, 31, **34**

headaches, 46

hemorrhages, 46

Justinian's plague, 12, 20–21

Kitasato, Shibasaburo, 13, 15, 30–31, 33

lymph nodes/buboes, **10**, 11, 14, 15, 46

medieval medicine, **5**, 21–23

Miles, Mary, 30

Ogata, Masanori, 33–34

pandemic in 1893, 12, 30

pandemic disease, definition of, 9

Pasteurella bacilla, 15

pets/dogs and cats, **5**, 17, 41

plague
causes of, 5–7, 11, 13, 14–15
history of, 19–31
modern treatment for, 47–49
pneumonic form of, 16, 47–48
prevention of, 51–55
symptoms of, 10–11, 16, 20, 37, 46

Index